ROY

A Life from Beginning to End

Copyright © 2023 by Hourly History.

All rights reserved.

Table of Contents

Introduction
Early Life in Texas
A Target for Bullies
Orbison and the Teen Kings
Breakthrough Hit
Triumph and Tragedy
A Decade of Decline
Emerging From Obscurity
Roy's Last Act: The Traveling Wilburys
Death and Aftermath
Conclusion
Bibliography

Introduction

Roy Kelton Orbison came into this world on April 23, 1936, the second of three children born by Orbie Lee and Nadine Vesta Orbison. The Orbisons lived in the quaint environs of Vernon, Texas, where family, church, and country meant just about everything. They would eventually pick up and move to the big city of Fort Worth in 1942 when Roy's father found work at an aircraft factory. The United States had just been drawn into World War II after all, so industrial plants cranking out armaments for the war did indeed need workers, and Mr. Orbison was ready to fit that bill. However, the family's urban life in Fort Worth was marred by the outbreak of polio, a disease that, at the time, posed a severe threat to life and limb. Fearing for their kids, the Orbisons soon sent them to live with Nadine's mother for safekeeping back in Vernon.

It was back here in Vernon that Roy Orbison first fell in love, for on his sixth birthday, he was gifted with a guitar. This event sparked a lifelong affair with music, and Roy dedicated himself to it from that point forward. His earliest musical inspiration was the Texas soundscape of the 1940s, which was predominantly country western music. Legends like Hank Williams, Moon Mullican, Jimmie Rogers, and Ernest Tubb greatly influenced Orbison's style, and he even had the opportunity to witness Tubb live, playing an impromptu gig from the back of a pickup truck.

As time went by, Orbison would also begin to broaden his horizons, taking in the growing rhythm and blues scene. His musical talents began to garner notice quite quickly, and in 1945, a nine-year-old Roy Orbison managed to make his way onto a radio show. From here on out, music was his muse, and he would never look back.

Chapter One

Early Life in Texas

"It's always been my nature to create music. It's always been a part of my life."

—Roy Orbison

After his debut on the radio, where he wowed radio listeners with a heartfelt rendition of "You Are My Sunshine," Orbison proved that he was not just a flash in the pan. The precocious kid with glasses had impressed the guys at the station enough for them to agree to give him a regular slot on Saturdays to sing any two songs he liked. Soon, Roy Orbison was regularly belting out traditional classics to radio listeners, such as the coalminers' anthem "Sixteen Tons."

In 1946, in the meantime, the burgeoning child prodigy Roy Orbison was on the move. That year, his family trundled him and his guitar up and moved themselves on over to Wink, Texas. Wink was a small oil town in the far reaches of western Texas where most of the population likely worked for the local oil refinery or were related to someone who did. Roy would later recall Wink as not exactly being music friendly. He would joke about the place as being the kind of Texas town which lived and breathed oil, football, and sand—but not a whole lot else.

As far as the Texan love for football goes, Roy Orbison, for his part, was never very athletic and likely wasn't about to get picked for the Wink Wildcat's varsity football team any time soon. Along with his lack of physical coordination, Roy Orbison also stood out for the fact that he wore thick glasses. The whole Orbison family, in fact, seemed to have bad eyesight, and from a young age, all of the Orbison kids wore thick, unsightly glasses on their faces. Such things certainly didn't do much to endear Roy to his more judgmental peers.

Roy's face was another thing that made him stand out since a childhood battle with jaundice left him with a permanently pale complexion. This was coupled with frizzy, dishwater blonde hair, which he started dying jet black at a fairly young age. Looking part Elvis and part goth, Orbison was in many ways a trailblazer, willing to do things that others were not, way ahead of any notable trends leading in that direction.

Nevertheless, no matter what he looked like, his voice would carry him a long way. Roy would bring his guitar to school with him and was often seen right in the middle of the school hallway, playing his guitar and singing his heart out.

It wasn't long before Orbison and some kids from Wink formed a band and began to perform together. Suitably enough, they called themselves the Wink Westerners. The name was apparently the idea of the boys' science teacher—Miss Hardin—but whatever the case was, the proffered moniker seemed to work. The repertoire of the group was indeed primarily western standards, but they occasionally threw some Glenn Miller songs into the mix to liven things up. Roy also took the time to write his own tunes—one of the earliest being a real crooner called "I Am Just a Dreamer."

Soon, Orbison and his Wink Westerners were playing at school events and even local establishments such as the Day Drug Store, where they performed for the drifters and rounders who happened to be lounging around there at the time. It was at the local drug store that these youngsters first got a taste of what it was like to be paid performers since after they played, they had several happy customers hand them a few dollars to show their appreciation.

And more was to come; as they expanded their scope to venues far and wide, they were given a gig to perform at the local Lions Club. It was here that the shocked youngsters were handed $400 for their performance—a great deal of money for nascent performers in West Texas back in the late 1940s.

Around this same time, the superintendent of Roy Orbison's school, a man whose name comes down to us as R. A. Lipscomb, took a liking to the band. Superintendent Lipscomb just so happened to be running for district governor of the Lions Club and decided to use Roy and the boys' musical outfit for his campaign. Lipscomb had the boys go out to Chicago with him so that they could play at the Lions Club convention being held there. To Orbison's delight, now he was not only getting paid for his music, but he was also going out on tour. At this fateful moment, the budding musician realized that he could not only play for fun but actually earn a livelihood from it.

Still, these dreams were quite a far way off, and during his school days, he largely remained a shy nobody who most simply ignored despite his growing musical prowess outside of class. The real star of the family at this time was actually Roy's brother, who had proven to be a tremendous athlete on the football field while Roy literally sat on the sidelines. Although he played in a band and had regular gigs on the side, in high school, Roy was really only known for a few things; he drew comical pictures for the school yearbook, and he played in the marching band. He was also known for smoking, which was considered a very rebellious thing for young people to do in West Texas back in those days. Roy had apparently picked up the habit from his friend Joe Ray Hammer and would continue to smoke upward of 80 cigarettes per day for much of the rest of his life. Indeed, many of his early days would be spent playing music, smoking, and daydreaming of what might become of his life.

Chapter Two

A Target for Bullies

"You can never know about your own destiny: are the people who are figured out, who saw in clarity, were they merely lucky? Chance is a major factor in life."

—Roy Orbison

Toward the end of his high school years, Roy Orbison had a hard time of things. He had become the favorite target of one of the school's worst bullies—the captain of the football team—who regularly taunted Roy over his appearance. This taunting resulted in Orbison gaining the rather unfortunate nickname of "Facetus."

In the pressure cooker of high school, youngsters who find themselves on the lower end of the totem pole have a few ways of dealing with schoolyard bullies, but primarily one either decides to stand up to them or to simply take their abuse. Roy chose the latter. He even tried to come to terms with the bullying by using humor to laugh at his own expense, as was evident when he made it a point to sign yearbooks not as Roy Orbison but as "Facetus." Yet even though Roy tried to make light of it, such things no doubt bothered him deep down and would leave him feeling self-conscious about his appearance for the rest of his life. Orbison would ultimately have the last laugh, however, because many years later, when his fellow high schoolers heard of the fortune and fame of Roy Orbison, they likely searched their yearbooks for a readily made autograph. To their chagrin, instead of finding that their yearbooks were signed by Roy Orbison, they were faced with a reminder of their own immaturity: "Facetus."

Although he was shunned by the popular kids in school, Orbison had developed his own core of friends who sympathized with his problems. Along with playing music with them, these guys would often head out with Roy to have a little fun on the road. Many of these road trips ended up in Mexico, and it would later be claimed that Roy and his high school friends often frequented some of the seedier joints just over the Mexican border. Here, Orbison could smoke as many cigarettes as he pleased, as well as indulge his passion with local ladies who didn't seem to mind Roy's glasses and pale face.

At any rate, despite some of the outward turbulence he faced, Orbison had the blueprints for his dream life inside of him, and he would continue to follow them. One of the major milestones along the way of building this dream came on April 16, 1954, when he was privy to see Elvis Presley for the first time. His father, old Orbie Lee, had driven him all the way to Dallas to see the king of rock and roll live at the Big D. Jamboree. The concert was staged at the 6,000-seat Sportatorium, which—as its name just might imply—typically showcased popular wrestling matches when stars like Elvis weren't in town.

Besides the thrill of seeing Elvis, Orbison was also looking forward to seeing the likes of Sonny James and Charline Arthur. Yet the figure that stood out the most for Roy was Hank Locklin, whose performance of "Danny Boy" seemed to stir something inside the beating heart of Roy Orbison. It showed Roy the power of emotional ballads, and he would long reprise this formula for future ballads of his own.

Later that year, Orbison graduated from high school. Although he had long been bitten by the music bug, like many youngsters, his parents likely wanted him to have a backup plan in the works. So, after his graduation, Roy Orbison was enrolled at North Texas State College in Denton. Here, he took up geology, hoping that his knowledge of the earth and its natural minerals would perhaps land him a job at an oil drilling refinery, should his plans in the music business never come to fruition. It was a clever and pragmatic enough approach, but fortunately for Orbison and all of us who have enjoyed his songs throughout the years, this particular backup plan would never have to be executed.

Chapter Three

Orbison and the Teen Kings

"I always felt like I was on the move, that I was going somewhere."

—Roy Orbison

In the fall of 1954, Roy Orbison arrived at the campus of North Texas State. Although he began his geology studies with enthusiasm, it wasn't long before he grew tired and weary of learning about rocks. Fortunately, he found a silver lining in his academic pursuits through a course in music, where he enjoyed learning some of the finer points of musical theory that had been lost on him before.

In his time away from school, Orbison also developed a new and unexpected hobby at a local pool hall. As it turns out, Orbison was great at shooting pool, despite his poor eyesight. He was so good, in fact, that he regularly made extra money from pool hustling. His success in this unexpected arena was likely attributed to his unassuming nature; most would have looked at the shy and timid Roy and dismissed him as an easy opponent, never suspecting his proficiency at the pool table. Yet even if he was quite good at sinking the eight-ball, his meek and mild exterior still proved problematic among the rough-and-tumble crowd he was surrounded by at the pool hall. Even if Roy beat someone at pool after all, it wouldn't do much for him if the loser refused to pay up. The fact that he couldn't always ensure he would be able to collect his winnings eventually prompted Roy to put the brakes on his pool hustling.

More fortuitous for Orbison during this period was his meeting of Pat Boone, a fellow student at North Texas State. Boone was already making waves in the music industry by way of his sanitized versions of rock and roll classics such as "Tutti Frutti." Boone was quite good at smoothing over much of rock's rough edges and making previously edgy tunes more palatable as family entertainment. As such, Orbison likely figured if Pat Boone could do it—then so could he.

Shortly after his return back to Wink for Christmas break, he began to employ his own milder rendition of the rock and roll hit "Shake, Rattle, and Roll." Orbison was able to take this riotous song, polish it off, and streamline it. This new rendition he and the Wink Westerners performed at a New Year's Eve dance to the crowd's great delight. The clunky rhythm of Roy Orbison's guitar won the night—and so did Roy's voice which developed a much more free and loose rock and roll swagger. Ironically, it was in his attempt to clean up rock and roll that Roy Orbison inadvertently let it all hang out.

His subsequent return to classes at North Texas State was a little less than thrilling. He tried his luck at American history and English literature before he decided that he simply wasn't college material. He also, more than likely, couldn't resist putting his full force behind his music, which was more easily accomplished if he wasn't obligated to study and go to classes. Whatever the case may be, Roy Orbison decided that he was done with school and dropped out without even bothering to take his final exams. Instead of a career as a geologist studying rocks, Orbison decided he would rather get his kicks playing rock music.

Orbison wasn't going back to Wink either. Instead, he hooked up with some college friends and moved into a place in nearby Odessa, Texas.

Of course, he needed to make money, and with no job prospects lined up, all he had was his music. This he aggressively pursued by getting his band up and running in Odessa and getting various gigs in and around town.

By this time, the Wink Westerners was no longer so country western anymore. Rather than country standards, they were more keen to play raw and uncut rock and roll. Since they didn't live in Wink and they didn't play western music, it was obvious that the group needed to get a new name for themselves. After much thought and deliberation, they settled on calling themselves the Teen Kings. It's somewhat ironic that these young men, who were all now leaving their teenage years behind, would dub themselves the kings of the teens, but since they were primarily still playing school dances and other events that youngsters of this age group frequented, they probably figured that this was the most marketable title to have.

At any rate, the original lineup of Roy Orbison's band was going through some changes too. His original bassist—Charles "Slob" Evans—had become an enlisted man in the Navy. This meant that a new bass player was in order. Roy convinced a friend of his, Jack Kennelly, to fill the spot. Never mind the fact that Jack had never played bass in his life, Roy was banking on his personality more than his musical skill. He was a good friend, and for Roy, he was the right fit even if it meant he would have to give Jack a crash course on how to play bass. Jack Kennelly would later recall that he more or less pretended to play during his first few gigs. Fortunately, he was a quick study and soon learned the bass well enough to keep up with the band in his own right.

With Kennelly in tow, the lineup at this point consisted of Orbison as lead singer and guitarist, Johnny Wilson on guitar and backing vocals, James Morrow on electric mandolin, and Billy Pat Ellis on drums. This proved to be a recipe for success since the band soon had a major breakthrough when they opened for none other than Chuck Berry at a gig held at the County Auditorium. Even with all of this local acclaim, however, these local legends often weren't being paid that well, and their bookings were at times few and far between. Often enough, it was feast or famine for Roy Orbison and the Teen Kings, and they were in serious need of routine work. Fortunately, they eventually found it in the form of a local car dealer who sponsored a radio show. The dealership was willing to pay the group a whopping $5 a week for performing on the program. It wasn't much, but it was at least a steady gig. It also allowed Roy Orbison to extend his reach, as he hit the airwaves with his own versions of already classic songs like "The Great Pretender" and the ever-raucous Little Richard hit "Tutti Frutti."

Roy Orbison had certainly come a long way since his debut on the radio as a nine-year-old, but even so, on his long road to success, there were still a little ways left to go.

Chapter Four

Breakthrough Hit

"I was frustrated as a singer for a long time, particularly when one of the songs I'd written became a big hit for someone else."

—Roy Orbison

It was from his perch in Odessa, Texas, that Roy Orbison first met Johnny Cash when the country/rock and roll legend toured the region from 1955 to 1956. It was Cash who first suggested that Orbison and company try their luck with famed music mogul Sam Phillips down at Sun Records. Phillips, of course, had famously signed Elvis Presley and had breathed life into Johnny Cash's career as well. Roy figured that if the goose was good for the rest of the rock and roll gander, then it was likely good for him as well, and so he took Cash up on his offer.

When he finally gained an audience with Sam Phillips, he was rejected by the mogul, with Sam trouncing his referral by Cash by flatly stating that he was the boss and Johnny Cash most certainly was not. Nevertheless, a short time later, when Sam Phillips heard a recording of Roy Orbison and his band performing a lively track called "Ooby Dooby," he changed his mind. Upon hearing the incredible sound that is Roy Orbison, Sam readily signed him and the Teen Kings for their first contract with a major record label.

In the meantime, Roy Orbison had struck up what amounted to his first serious relationship by way of one Claudette Frady. Frady would be the great love of Orbison's life and also the source of great tragedy, with her untimely passing in 1966. Many of his songs would be written about Claudette, and she would serve as his muse well after she was gone. Orbison's attachment to his first true love, Claudette, could be said to demonstrate a noble sense of loyalty in Roy's overall character. No matter what else may have happened in their lives in between, since Claudette was there with Roy when he first rose to the top, she always meant a lot to him.

At any rate, after getting signed with Sun Records, Orbison and his band were soon on their way to Sun Studio in Memphis, Tennessee. Here, they were booked, at Phillips' request, to record that catchy track "Ooby Dooby" as soon as possible. It's said that the road trip out to the studio was a mini-adventure in itself. One can only imagine the feelings of this carload of young men as they drove off to meet their destiny. Excitement must have been in the air as their dreams finally seemed to be within their grasp.

The group's car pulled up in Sun Studio's parking lot on March 27, 1956, and the group immediately got to work. "Ooby Dooby" was recorded without a hitch, and the song would then begin its first round of circulation on radio stations that May. It was well received and reached the 59th spot on the Billboard chart. Greatly encouraged by this early success, Orbison and his band went back to the studio and began refining some more rousing rockabilly tunes, such as "Rockhouse" and the ever-engaging "Go! Go! Go!" Soon enough, though, the band members' egos began to get in the way.

Previously, like a bunch of musical musketeers, it had been all for one and one for all, but now open arguments were breaking out over just who should get credit for what and how much royalties each band member should receive for the individual contributions that they had made. These problems proved insurmountable, leading to the band's breakup before the end of the year. Nevertheless, even though his band had split, Roy Orbison wasn't going anywhere. He had already tasted success, and band or no band, he wasn't about to give it up. He remained right where he was in Memphis, and soon he was reaching out to Claudette to ask her to come up and join him.

Roy was actually staying in Sam Phillips' home at the time, and although Phillips let Claudette join Roy, he had them sleep in separate rooms until they got married. The couple's wedding day then came shortly thereafter in the summer of 1957. Not giving much time for a honeymoon, Orbison was writing up a storm during this period and managed to write a song that would be a hit for the Everly Brothers. The song was about his girl Claudette and was named as such in her honor.

Roy Orbison first met the Everly Brothers in early 1958 at a gig in Hammond, Indiana. The two musical outfits apparently got along well enough and befriended each other, and this friendship led Orbison to offer them what would become a major hit. Roy Orbison may not have had the joy of becoming the one famous for crooning this song, but the royalties he received as a songwriter were enough to get him through the night. Facing mounting frustration with Sun

Records in the meantime, his recordings soon came to a standstill and then simply ceased altogether. He went out on a brief tour, but becoming increasingly discouraged with the music scene, he ended up dropping out altogether for a number of months.

Realizing that songwriting was a true talent of his, he instead decided to throw himself into the songwriting business full-time, taking up a gig at Acuff-Rose. Acuff-Rose was a company that focused primarily on writing country music. By this time, Roy's wife had given birth to their first child—Roy DeWayne Orbison—in 1958. The couple had moved into their own apartment too, but the space for this growing family was quite limited, and Roy often escaped to the solitude of his car to write his songs.

Interestingly enough, fellow songwriter Joe Melson stumbled upon Orbison writing and playing guitar in his car, and after tapping on the window of his vehicle, he and Orbison began to collaborate and write songs together. Out of this material, Orbison would record a total of seven songs under the aegis of the record label RCA Victor, but only two of the recordings would be used by the label. It was a tough row for Roy Orbison to hoe, but he would ultimately come out on top, for it was in 1960 that he would have his break-out hit, "Only the Lonely."

Interestingly, Roy had initially tried to sell the song to other recording greats like the Everly Brothers and even Elvis Presley, but he was turned down. Instead, he ended up recording the song for himself, and the world would be glad that he did. It was truly only the haunting voice of Roy Orbison who could capture the words and feeling of this lonesome and lonely track. The song reached number two in the United States and soared all the way to the top in the United Kingdom and Australia. "Only the Lonely" proved that as good of a songwriter as Roy Orbison was, he was also quite the performer.

Chapter Five

Triumph and Tragedy

"You have to go through the falling down in order to learn to walk. It helps to know that you can survive it."

—Roy Orbison

The Roy Orbison hit "Only the Lonely" arrived at just the right time. In the year 1960, music was very much at a crossroads. The 1950s rock and roll era of Elvis was over, and Presley himself wasn't even in the country. He had enlisted in the U.S. armed forces and had been sent off to a U.S. army base in West Germany. At this point in time, it seemed that one era of music had ended, yet the era of the Beatles, the Rolling Stones, and Bob Dylan had not quite begun. The music world, as it were, was in a transitional no man's land when the music of Roy Orbison first became well known. Hits like "Only the Lonely," "Crying," and "Running Scared" would rise up the charts and simultaneously find a place in the hearts of countless young people desperately looking for something new during a time of uncertainty.

The song "Running Scared" was a rather whimsical yet poignant piece speaking of new romance and the fear of an old flame returning to snuff out the sparks that had just been kindled. This song perhaps could serve as a metaphor for Roy Orbison's musical career at this point since he had kindled something good musically speaking and had won over a sizeable musical audience that used to fawn over Elvis and the other pre-Orbison rock and roll giants. Having that said, perhaps Roy Orbison was subconsciously afraid the previous rock and roll greats just might come back to reclaim some of the fame they had lost. Whatever the case may be, "Running Scared" ultimately reached the number one spot on the charts. More hits were then soon to come in the form of classic tunes such as "In Dreams," "Blue Bayou," and the ever-catchy "Candy Man."

Roy, in the meantime, had become a father for a second time in 1962, when his son Anthony was born. He just barely had the time to take it all in before he was back out on tour the following year, and this particular tour wasn't just any old tour for that fateful year of 1963 was when the Beatles landed and the British invasion began. The Beatles—John, Paul, George, and Ringo—ushered in the new sound and the next evolution of rock and roll that everyone seemed to be waiting for. It was Roy Orbison, who somehow seemed to serve as both a bridge to the past and the future, who was recruited to go on tour with them.

While Orbison was out on the road with the Beatles, he began to develop his image as a performing artist. His signature look—those iconic Wayfarer sunglasses coupled with his black clothing and dyed black hair—was actually born out of a bit of a mishap. He wasn't initially trying to cultivate a mysterious stage persona; it happened more by accident. The story goes that, while on tour in England with the Beatles, Orbison misplaced his regular prescription glasses on an airplane. The only ones he had on hand were a pair of prescription sunglasses. Without any other option, he decided to wear these sunglasses on stage for his performance.

To his surprise, the look was well-received. The sunglasses, combined with his usual attire of black clothing, gave him an air of mystery and uniqueness that stood out in the music industry. Recognizing this, he decided to keep wearing the sunglasses on stage, turning what was originally a practical solution into a significant part of his public image. They also helped him manage his stage fright, as they served as a sort of barrier between him and the audience and made the usually shy and introverted Orbison feel more comfortable while performing.

It's also said that during the tour with the Beatles, there was initially some conflict due to the competing egos of the musicians. John Lennon, in particular, was apparently irked that Orbison did so many encores, thereby eating into the Beatles' time on stage. At one point, it's said that Lennon and McCartney even laid hands on Orbison just to keep him from going out on stage again. It's hard to imagine John Lennon and Paul McCartney resorting to physical force to deter their tour mate, but according to several different sources on the subject, it's said that such a thing really did occur. Nevertheless, before it was all over with, they all became the best of friends. Roy had become particularly fond of the Beatles' lead guitar player George Harrison, which would lead many years later to the creation of the epic supergroup known as the Traveling Wilburys.

Yet as much fun as he was having on the road, Orbison's home life was in turmoil. His wife Claudette, tired of being left at home all by herself waiting on Roy, ended up having an affair with a contractor who was working on building them a house in Hendersonville, Tennessee. As devastating as all this no doubt was, it couldn't be kept secret, and soon Roy would find out all about it. He was, of course, heartbroken, but nevertheless, he and Claudette eventually managed to patch things up and reconcile their differences.

Once back in the States, Roy Orbison would manage to crank out another major hit with the rendering of the unforgettable track "Oh, Pretty Woman." The song was about his wife Claudette, both a tribute to her as well as an emotional take on the push and pull between them. It's said that the song was inspired when Claudette, in a huff, suddenly announced that she was going to Nashville. Roy was working on writing songs with a guy named Bill Dees at the time, and upon hearing her announcement that she was leaving, he asked her if she had any cash to get to Nashville. It was then Bill Dees bluntly remarked, "A pretty woman never needs any money."

This line was what kicked off the songwriting process that led to "Oh, Pretty Woman." The song was a number-one hit for Roy Orbison even during the height of Beatlemania and would remain a high point of his career. Yet even with this success, the turmoil with Claudette would continue, and the couple would divorce in November of 1964 in light of new infidelities. They would get back together the following year, and this reconciliation was seemingly solidified in the form of a new child, for in 1965, Claudette gave birth to a son named Wesley.

By this time, Roy Orbison had gotten a deal with MGM, and with them, he would release a whole slew of new albums, but most of them were rather forgettable. It's not to say that Roy Orbison didn't craft any good songs—he certainly did. Some even made some headway in Britain and Australia, but nevertheless, for the most part, his new material was simply not produced or marketed well enough for the wider audience to know much about it. As a result, his work increasingly slipped into obscurity.

An entirely unexpected tragedy would then strike when Orbison was out riding motorcycles with Claudette in Bristol, Tennessee. Both Roy and Claudette were avid motorcycle enthusiasts and enjoyed nothing more than riding down the open road on their bikes with the wind in their hair. On June 6, 1966, however, their sojourn would be tragically interrupted when 25-year-old Claudette suffered a head-on collision with a truck. She died at the scene. Despite any previous problems they might have had, this was the end of the greatest love of Orbison's life. Roy Orbison—the man of mystery—would retreat into the shadows even further after this.

Chapter Six
A Decade of Decline

"I may be a living legend, but that sure don't help when I've got to change a flat tire."

—Roy Orbison

Roy Orbison was in many ways a lost man after his wife Claudette died. At first, he tried to immerse himself in his music in order to not think about the pain he felt. It was these efforts of a deeply grieving man that would produce *The Classic Roy Orbison* album that came out before that fateful year of 1966 was through. It's interesting to note that although Orbison's career was by no means over, it was as if he already felt it was coming to an end. Most artists don't start viewing their work as "classic" until they are near retirement.

The photos of Orbison for this record perhaps tell the story of his mental state even more than the songs themselves. Here, he truly looks like a man in mourning, completely detached from the world. He's decked out in black clothes and black sunglasses, with his signature dyed black hair to match. His face is also quite serious, perhaps even a bit menacing. He seems to be a man lost in his own anguish, contemplating the destruction of all he has known before. He gazes back in time, even as he considers what could have been.

Music in general was indeed changing greatly during this period, so perhaps it could be said that Roy was quite prescient to dub his tunes as classics since he sensed that the music world was on the verge of a major change. The early 1960s that saw him rise to prominence had now morphed into the late 1960s, and 1967 and 1968 would certainly be a lot different from 1963 and even 1964. Now it was edgy acts such as the Doors and Jimi Hendrix who stole the show, and Roy Orbison's romantic ballads would seem decidedly out of place and dated, as if they were from another era altogether.

It was just as he was struggling to find his footing in the changing world of music that Orbison's life was rocked once again by yet another terrible tragedy. On September 14, 1968, while he was out on tour in Europe, he learned that his house in Hendersonville had caught on fire and burnt to the ground. Tragically, his two oldest sons perished in this terrible inferno. His youngest son Wesley managed to survive, but the grief-stricken Roy Orbison, apparently unable to tend to him, would ultimately leave his care in the hands of his parents. Wesley would grow up raised by his grandparents, as his own father seemed to become increasingly distant.

Orbison ended up selling the property to his old friend Johnny Cash. Cash cleared out all the burned-up rubble, but refusing to build on the site where Roy's kids had perished, he decided to plant an orchard there instead. Orbison, in the meantime, had met a young woman named Barbara while he was on tour in Britain. Although Barbara met him at a nightclub in West Yorkshire, England, she was not British but originally hailed from Germany in the West German town of Bielefeld, to be exact.

Barbara was only 18 years old when she met the then 32-year-old Roy, but despite their age difference, they apparently hit it off quite well together. Orbison brought her back to the States with him, and on March 25, 1969, the two were married. This union would later produce two more sons for Roy Orbison—Roy Kelton, born in 1970, and Alexander, born in 1975. It was the same year that baby Roy was born in 1970 that

Orbison managed to squeak out an overseas smash hit.

Although it didn't make waves in the U.S., the single "Penny Arcade" shot to number one in Australia and remained there for some time. This song was from the Orbison album released that same year entitled *The Big O*. The title of the album was actually inspired by a nickname that Orbison had picked up when a DJ who was fond of Orbison's big dramatic finishes began calling him "The Big O." By the time Roy's son Alexander was born in 1975, however, his career was once again in decline. That year, Orbison released a record of romantic tunes called *I'm Still in Love with You*, but at this point, his career had clearly flopped, and he had not had a hit song in several years. Many of his albums, in fact, were not even released internationally since they failed to sell in the United States.

Orbison had left MGM by this time and had begun experimenting with other outlets. Despite his decline in the charts, he was still a popular pop culture figure, and he was especially revered among other musicians who routinely covered his previous hit songs. In the late 1970s, he even began touring with big-name rock bands of the time—most notably the Eagles in 1976. That same fateful year, Orbison released a new album that he hoped would revive his career. The new record was named, aptly enough, *Regeneration*. Unfortunately, though, even this attempt at a comeback proved to be somewhat lacking in its execution. Here, Roy Orbison belted out some heartfelt tracks such as "I'm a Southern Man" and "Something They Can't Take Away," but it all somehow fell flat and failed to make any headway on the music charts.

Defeated and dejected, Roy Orbison's very health began to decline. He had gone on a brief vacation to the Hawaiian Islands in 1977, only to fall ill. After heading to the hospital, he was found to have severe blockages in his coronary arteries. This resulted in a triple bypass surgery, which was conducted on January 18, 1978. It would take Roy Orbison some time to recover, and over the next couple of years, he would largely put his music career on hold.

Chapter Seven

Emerging From Obscurity

"If you have faith, then your whole life is put in a new perspective. You get to work but enjoy the work at the same time. If you grow spiritually, you do what's in front of you and let the results speak for themselves."

—Roy Orbison

After recovering from deteriorating health and dwindling record sales in the late 1970s, Roy Orbison found that the early 1980s were not exactly welcoming to his brand of music. Even so, he was able to make a brief comeback of sorts in 1981, when he and country music star Emmylou Harris managed to win a Grammy Award for a duet they performed of "That Lovin' You Feelin' Again." It was just a small glimmer of Roy Orbison's past greatness, but it was enough for the aging star to be able to peek through the cracks and once again see the possibilities of what he could do in the music world.

Tributes continued to pour in, for it was the following year of 1982 that Roy Orbison was flattered to find that none other than the hard-driving rock group Van Halen had covered "Oh, Pretty Woman" on their masterwork album *Diver Down*. There was some turbulence ahead, however, when the following year, Orbison came into a terrible dispute with his old songwriting company Acuff-Rose. Orbison, who had lent his talent to Acuff-Rose since 1958, had come to the conclusion that he wasn't being treated properly by upper management and accused them of fraudulent business practices. Orbison ended up filing a lawsuit against Acuff-Rose to the tune of some $50 million. Some of the finer details of this case are still obscure, but it seems that Roy and his old partners at Acuff-Rose ultimately decided to settle their differences out of court in exchange for $3 million.

Roy Orbison seemed to be at a crossroads in both his life and his career at this time, and looking for a change, he decided to pick up from where he had been living in Tennessee and move on over to California. He arrived in Southern California in 1985, and according to his spouse

Barbara, he was ready to hit the ground running. According to her, Roy was well aware that he was almost 50 years old, and knowing that he wasn't getting any younger, he was determined to revive his career. The first step in this process of revitalization seemed to emerge in 1986 when his song "In Dreams" was used in the David Lynch film *Blue Velvet*. This seemed to set the stage for Roy Orbison's greatest hits album in 1987, which was dubbed *In Dreams: The Greatest Hits*.

The year of 1987 could be said to kick off Orbison's great era of collaboration. That year, he made songs with a multitude of artists. At one point, he even co-wrote some material with Glenn Danzig, the frontman of hard rockers the Misfits. Orbison was indeed finally receiving some much overdue recognition, and that same year, he even managed to obtain his induction into the Rock and Roll Hall of Fame and the Nashville Songwriters Hall of Fame. It was one of the great highlights of his career and had the aging rock and roller introduced to the gathered crowd by none other than Bruce Springsteen.

A few months later, Springsteen, Bonnie Raitt, and many other notable performers hooked up with Roy Orbison for a televised performance called *Roy Orbison and Friends: A Black and*

White Night. The musicians performed at Los Angeles' Ambassador Hotel in the Coconut Grove Ballroom. The performers played into the night, spanning some four hours' worth of material. The performance was not only popular then but would remain a cult favorite as it was routinely rebroadcast over the years.

Yet it was when Orbison began collaborating with Jeff Lynne, the frontman of Electric Light Orchestra, and his old pal from the Beatles, George Harrison, in 1988 that some truly incredible things began to occur. The three men began to regularly hang out and write songs together. Before long, they hooked up with their mutual friend Bob Dylan, who had the whole crew come over to his home to record some of the material they had come up with. George Harrison was also good friends with rocker Tom Petty, and it wasn't long before Petty was tapped to join the sessions as well.

It was this formation of star power that would lead to the creation of the supergroup called the Traveling Wilburys, with Roy Orbison dubbing himself "Lefty Wilbury" in honor of an old hero of his—country western singer Lefty Frizzell. With the Wilbury lineup complete, Roy Orbison's last great act had begun.

Chapter Eight

Roy's Last Act: The Traveling Wilburys

"It's very nice to be wanted again, but I still can't quite believe it."

—Roy Orbison

Roy Orbison put his heart and soul into the star-studded musical collaborative project known as the Traveling Wilburys. All of his bandmates for this project were just as famous as he was, yet they couldn't help but be mesmerized by Roy's powerful voice and his stature in the business, as well as his own personal work ethic. Jeff Lynne later spoke of the recording sessions, saying, "Everybody just sat there going, 'Wow it's Roy Orbison!' Even though he's become your pal and you're hanging out and having a laugh and going to dinner, as soon as he gets behind that [mic] and he's doing his business, suddenly it's shudder time."

During production, all members of the Traveling Wilburys became the best of friends. Their recording sessions—although taken very seriously—had the vibe of a group of buddies getting together to hang out. All of the Wilburys seemed to be on the same page, and disagreements were minimal; if any were to surface, they typically solved them by way of a group vote. Incredibly enough, it only took six weeks to produce this record, and the group's album, simply dubbed *Traveling Wilburys Vol. 1*, made its debut on October 25, 1988. Rock critics hailed it as a masterpiece almost immediately, and rock music fans weighed in by buying up the album in the droves. The first single from the album—"Handle With Care"—soared up the charts and immediately became a radio favorite.

Although group members were credited on every song for their general contribution, they were also given time to showcase their own unique talent. As it pertains to Orbison, this album featured a solo track by Roy entitled "Not Alone Any More." This song had Orbison going back to his roots as the master of sad and heartwarming tunes. While everyone was impressed with Roy's delivery, Lynne found himself less than thrilled with some of the backing instrumentation. As such, he ended up re-doing much of the instrumental takes himself at the last minute. The result was very well-received, and the song is often cited by fans and critics as a highlight of the album.

Taking full advantage of his revived career, Orbison, in the meantime, produced a new solo album, which he called *Mystery Girl*. Yes, the man of mystery Roy Orbison had returned, and now he was writing a full, feature-length album about his "mystery girl." This album was also produced by fellow Wilbury Jeff Lynne. The album had several memorable tracks. The song "She's a Mystery to Me" was actually one that had been originally penned by Bono and Edge from the pop/rock band U2. The song contained many metaphors and powerful bits of imagery that Roy Orbison seemed to use to great effect.

Yet while Orbison was doing well as far as music was concerned, his health was once again causing him trouble. By this point, he had begun complaining of chest pains, as it seemed that his old heart problems from a decade prior were making a return. Nevertheless, Orbison refused to slow down; he worked hard in the studio and hard on the road. He went out on tour, played sold-out concerts, and gave countless interviews. Little did anyone know that this was Roy

Orbison's last great gasp. Sadly enough, just as many were finally getting reacquainted with his work, the world would be rocked by Roy Orbison's sudden passing on December 6, 1988.

Chapter Nine

Death and Aftermath

"People often ask me how would I like to be remembered, and I answer that I would simply like to be remembered."

—Roy Orbison

Coming off of his busy schedule of touring, Orbison had flown home to Hendersonville, Tennessee, on December 4, 1988. He was supposed to take it easy and rest up before he needed to drive off to the airport and fly to London, where he and his fellow Wilburys were scheduled to shoot some videos. On December 6, it's said that he spent the early part of the day hanging out with his chauffeur and friend Benny Birchfield, with whom he had a shared passion for model airplanes. The two had, in fact, spent several hours flying model planes together before having dinner and calling it a day. After saying goodbye to Benny, Orbison then went off to his mother's house to pay her a visit. It was here, with his mom at his side, that the then 52-year-old Roy Orbison succumbed to a fatal heart attack.

His death came as a shock to many since, at this point in his life, he seemed healthier than he had ever been. He had lost weight and was eating much healthier than he had ever been since he had been on a strict diet leading up to the release of the Wilburys album. Besides smoking, he also did not suffer from the usual rockstar vices such as drug or alcohol addiction. Many who saw him at his last concerts, right before his passing, would walk away speaking of just how healthy and robust he seemed.

At any rate, after his untimely demise, there would be endless praise, posthumous awards, tributes, and even concerts held in his honor. In one tribute concert held shortly after his death, none other than country music legend Bonnie Raitt was heard on stage singing the praises of Roy Orbison. Raitt gushed that there was simply no one out there who could quite compare to the natural musical force that had been summoned by Roy Orbison. But perhaps the greatest tribute to Roy Orbison of all was the fact that upon his passing, he became the first artist since Elvis to have two different records reach the top five on the album charts at the same time.

By April of 1989, Roy's last album *Mystery Girl* had reached the number five spot, and his record with the *Traveling Wilburys* had hit number four—certainly not a bad final send-off for the Big O by any stretch of the imagination. The second single from the *Traveling Wilburys*, a piece entitled "End of the Line," was also making major headway on radio stations. The irony of the title was not lost on many, and the video for the piece also managed to capture the finality of Roy Orbison's life since it was put together just a few days after he died. Since Orbison obviously wasn't available for the filming, the surviving members simply put a framed picture of Orbison behind an old rocking chair, which the camera would zoom in on from time to time. This certainly added a haunting quality to the track, but nevertheless, it was still quite well-received by critics and fans alike.

There was more to come, however, when in 1992, another Roy Orbison record was released posthumously entitled *King of Hearts*. This record was made up of all previously unreleased material and proved to be a real treasure trove for Orbison fans. The album was well received, despite the negative connotations that are often attached to posthumous albums. Orbison was very prodigious in his last few years of life, so there was indeed a great wealth of unused material to choose from. As such, this album was not so much the scraps that Roy Orbison had left behind as they were the final hidden gems that needed to be dug up and brought forth to see the light of day.

This was in no small part due to the efforts of Roy's widow Barbara, who not only dutifully stuck to Roy Orbison's side in life but also in death. After Roy's passing, Barbara would serve as the steward of his estate and the protector of his musical legacy. She even formed a record label in honor of her late husband called Orbison Records. It was through this label that she directed the release of previously unknown live material called *Combo Concert*, which came out in January of 1998. The recordings date back to Roy's time touring France and the Netherlands in his heyday in 1965.

Barbara did indeed do all she could to keep Roy's legacy alive until her own passing in December of 2011. She was suffering from an advanced stage of pancreatic cancer, which was first discovered the previous May. Strangely enough, she passed away on the same day her husband did, on December 6, and after she passed, Roy's estate fell into the hands of Roy and Barbara's sons, Roy Kelton and Alexander.

Conclusion

Roy Orbison was indeed a rare, enigmatic character. As some music journalists have noted throughout the years, the most intriguing thing about Roy Orbison is the fact that we don't know a whole lot about him. We might know his songs and the basic rudiments of his life story, but unlike other big-time stars who have gone on the record to state their likes and dislikes of just about everything under the sun, the personal views and opinions of Roy Orbison have largely remained hidden.

It's been said that although everyone routinely asked celebrities such as Elvis Presley and John Lennon what they thought about things such as the Vietnam War, religion, and anything else viewed with any significance, no one thought to ask Roy! It was likely due to his quiet, reserved demeanor that most didn't even bother to question him too much. A lot of the time, the press seemed to count themselves lucky just to get a glimpse of the quiet mystery man and didn't bother delving too deep into what the man behind the dark glasses actually thought. It seems that it was only after his passing that many began to realize the lost opportunity of actually getting to know the man behind the mystery.

Orbison's introspective nature no doubt veiled the passionate spirit that fueled his music. His distinctive voice, combined with his knack for writing heart-wrenching songs, set him apart from his contemporaries and continues to resonate with people to this day. It is the universal language of emotion, delivered through the irreplaceable voice of Roy Orbison.

Bibliography

Clayson, Alan (1989). *Only the Lonely: Roy Orbison's Life and Legacy.*

DeCurtis, Anthony; Henke, James (1992). *The Rolling Stone Illustrated History of Rock & Roll.*

Lehman, Peter (2003). *Roy Orbison:* The Invention of An Alternative Rock Masculinity.

Orbison, Roy, Jr; Orbison, Wesley; Orbison, Alex; Slate, Jeff (2017). *The Authorized Roy Orbison.*

Thomas, Nick (2017). *The Traveling Wilburys: The Biography.*

Roy Orbison Official Website. https://www.royorbison.com/

Printed in Dunstable, United Kingdom